A First Look
THE CHRISTIAN LIFE

Lois Rock

Illustrated by Carolyn Cox

Educational consultant: Margaret Dean

A LION BOOK

Bible passages mentioned in this book:

1 Luke, chapter 18, verses 9 to 14
2 Romans, chapter 4, verse 25 to chapter 5, verse 1
3 Isaiah, chapter 43 verses 1 to 5
4 Matthew, chapter 22, verse 37
5 1 John, chapter 4, verse 21 to chapter 5, verse 4
6 Matthew, chapter 5, verse 43 to 48
7 1 Corinthians, chapter 13, verse 4 to 5
8 1 Corinthians, chapter 13, verse 6
9 1 Corinthians, chapter 13, verse 7
10 1 Corinthians, chapter 15, verse 12 to 28
11 1 Timothy, chapter 6, verses 17 to 19
12 1 Peter, chapter 3, verses 14 to 16
13 1 Corinthians, chapter 13, verses 8 to 13

Text by Lois Rock
Copyright © 1996 Lion Publishing
Illustrations copyright © 1996 Carolyn Cox

The author asserts the moral right
to be identified as the author of this work

Published by
Lion Publishing plc
Sandy Lane West, Oxford, England
ISBN 0 7459 3187 1
Albatross Books Pty Ltd
PO Box 320, Sutherland, NSW 2232, Australia
ISBN 0 7324 0983 7

First edition 1996
10 9 8 7 6 5 4 3 2 1 0

A catalogue record for this book is available
from the British Library

Printed and bound in Singapore

Contents

Introduction
What is
The Christian life?

A Christian is someone who follows the example of Jesus Christ.

Jesus: the Christmas baby.

When he grew up, he told people how to live as God's friends: loving God and one another. And that's how he lived his life.

He even forgave the people who hurt him and killed him.

And then God gave him new life—new life with God for ever.

Christians believe they can have a new kind of life too.

In this book you will discover some of the things they believe about what makes the Christian life special:

● faith: trusting that Jesus has mended the friendship with God

● hope: looking forward to a new life with God for ever—a life that death cannot beat

● love: knowing God's love and care that will last for ever; learning to love God and other people.

1 Let's look at
Needing help

Imagine: you had this really great plan. You knew everything you needed to know. You could do it all. But now things aren't working. You need help.

Christians believe that everyone is a bit like that. They believe that, from the beginning, people have followed their own plans. They have turned away from the God who made them. They have broken the friendship with God.

To begin to live as a Christian is to see that those plans aren't working, and to ask God to help.

'Once,' said Jesus, 'two people went to the Temple to pray. One told God all the wonderful things he'd done. The other knew he had failed to live as God wants. "God, have pity on me," he said. 'I tell you,' said Jesus, 'it was the one who asked for God's help who was put right with God when he went home.'

From the book Luke wrote about Jesus.

To live the Christian life, a person needs to ask for God's help.

2 Let's look at

Trust

Do you sometimes stop being friends with someone? How do you put things right?

Sometimes another person says they will help. 'Follow me,' they say. 'I've put everything right.' Do you trust them? Do you have faith in what they say?

Christians believe that Jesus was God's son. They believe he came to mend the broken friendship between God and people, to show people that God still loved them. So Christians trust Jesus: they must have faith in what he did and what he said.

Here is what one of the first Christians said:

'Jesus has done all that is needed to make things right between us and God. If we have faith in what Jesus has done, then the friendship is mended. That makes us truly happy.'

From the letter Paul wrote to the first Christians in Rome

To live the Christian life, a person has faith in Jesus to take them back to God.

3 Let's look at
Names

Imagine!
The person you admire
most in the whole world
is coming—coming to
see you.
They know your name.
They must think you're
very important too!

Christians believe that the God who made everything in the whole wide world loves every single person.
They believe God knows everyone by their name.
They believe God wants to be friends with everyone.

God says this to people:
Do not be afraid: I have called you by name—you are mine. And you are very precious to me.
From the book of Isaiah in the Bible

To live the Christian life, a person needs to know just how much God loves them.

4 Let's look at
Being loved

How good it is to be loved...
When someone loves you even
when you're in a mess, puts
everything right, and doesn't
say a word about the rotten
things you did. It's easy to love
someone who loves you like
that.

Christians say they have found out how much God loves them. Their lives are changed. They want to do what Jesus told them more than anything else:

> *'Love the Lord your God with all your heart, and with all your soul, and with all your mind.'*

From the book Matthew wrote about Jesus

To live the Christian life, a person will make loving God the most important thing in life.

5 Let's look at
An overflowing cup

You asked for a drink...
it's delicious... and now the person pouring is offering more and more and more!

Quick, everyone, come round and share what I'm being given!

When Christians know they are loved by God more than they will ever know, their life is like a cup running over with love. They want most of all to share that love with others.

Jesus told us this: 'Whoever loves God must love other people too... and do all the things God has told us.'

From the first letter Jesus' friend, John, wrote to new Christians

To live the Christian life, a person will show love to others in everything they do.

6 Let's look at
Enemies

Here comes your worst enemy. What are you going to do: fight? run? hide? Have you got any other ideas?

Christians will remember what Jesus said:

'Love your enemies. Ask God to show kindness to those who go out their way to hurt you.'

From the book Matthew wrote about Jesus

After all, God is generous to everyone said Jesus, sending sunshine and rain to good people and to bad people.

To live the Christian life, a person learns to love as perfectly as God loves—and that includes loving their enemies.

7 Let's look at
Kindness

A person who loves you ought to be kind.

Christians believe that their love for others should be like God's love for them: always kind, patient and forgiving. They do not find it easy to love in this way, and sometimes they fail. But they do not give up trying, and they ask God to help them.

Love is patient and kind. It is not jealous or stuck up in any way. It is not rude or selfish or cross. It doesn't keep going on and on about all the bad things done in the past.

From Paul's first letter to the Christians in Corinth, from the Bible

To live the Christian life, a person will try to be patient and kind and forgiving.

8 Let's look at
A spoiled garden

A garden should be a place to play—not a place where people get hurt! Just look at all the things that spoil it. If only you could get rid of them.

Christians are sad and angry about the bad things that spoil the world: the quarrelling that spoils friendships, the fighting that leaves people hurt, the unfair grabbing that makes some people rich and others poor, the greedy snatching at all the planet has to offer.

Christian love isn't a soft kind of thing.

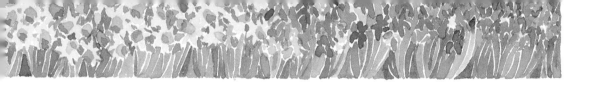

Love is not happy with evil, bad things. It wants to put things right, so they are as God first planned them to be.

From Paul's first letter to the Christians in Corinth from the Bible

To live the Christian life, a person will try to set bad things right.

9 Let's look at
One last chance

You did it wrong *again*.
Will you be punished?
Oh dear. It's like living
under a huge black cloud.

Christians know how hard it is to do the things that are right. They know they often fail.

And they know that God loves and forgives them over and over again.

So they want to be like that with other people, and with the things they want to see put right.

Love never gives up.

From Paul's first letter to the Christians in Corinth, from the Bible.

To live the Christian life, a person will go on loving for ever—as God does.

Planting seeds

Have you ever sown seeds? Some are so tiny! Will they be lost for ever when you scatter them on the soil?

You just have to hope they will grow. Everything you know about seeds tells you that they will.

Christians have faith that Jesus makes them God's friends. Everything they know about God and Jesus gives them hope that this friendship will last for ever.

God raised Jesus from death. One day, God promises, all Jesus' followers will be raised to new life too. Jesus will be their king, for ever.

From Paul's first letter to the Christians in Corinth, from the Bible

To live the Christian life, a person will place their hope in God, trusting God's promises for the future.

11 Let's look at Something worth having

Sometimes you want a thing so badly. You save and save, and wait and wait, and go without other presents... and then you have it.

Suddenly, it doesn't seem so important after all. Was it really worth all that effort to get?

Christians believe that doing what
God wants gives them something
worth having.

*Even if you're rich in money,
don't put your hope for a
happy future in that.
Your hope is really for a life
with Jesus for ever. So get
ready for that. Make yourself
rich in good works. Be
generous and ready to
share with others. In this way,
you will be storing up lasting
treasure.*

**From Paul's first letter to
Timothy, from the Bible**

**To live the Christian life, a
person will place their hope
in a future with Jesus, and in
doing the good things that
will be worth something then.**

12 Let's look at
Happiness that shows

When life is hard, people don't expect you to look happy.

But if you know that the hard times will soon be over, your happiness will show.

Christians believe they have good news: one day they will be with Jesus for ever. However bad things get, they go on hoping—and it shows.

Here is what Peter, one of Jesus' closest friends, said:

Even if you face hard times now for being a Christian, you still have a reason to be happy. Jesus is really in charge, and that gives you hope. Be ready at all times to explain why Jesus gives you hope. And when you do, be gentle, and show respect to the other person.

From the letter Peter wrote to the first Christians, from the Bible

To live the Christian life, a person needs to be ready at all times to explain why Jesus gives them hope even through the hard times.

13 Let's look at
Things that last

Worn out clothes...
worn out shoes...
worn out toys...
Does anything last for
ever?

Christians know that
things don't last.
So what does?

Here is what Paul, one of the first Christians, said:

Love lasts for ever. Right now, we only understand a little bit of what God is like. What we glimpse can seem very important and exciting, but it's nothing compared with seeing God face to face.
The three things that really matter in our lives are faith and hope in God, and love.

And love is what matters most of all.

From Paul's first letter to the Christians in Corinth, from the Bible

The Christian life is based on three things: faith in God, hope for a future with God, and God's great love, to enjoy and to share.

What is the Christian life?

1   To live the Christian life, a person needs to ask for God's help.

2   To live the Christian life, a person has faith in Jesus to take them back to God.

3   To live the Christian life, a person needs to know just how much God loves them.

4   To live the Christian life, a person will make loving God the most important thing in life.

5   To live the Christian life, a person will show love to others in everything they do.

6   To live the Christian life, a person learns to love as perfectly as God loves—and that includes loving their enemies.

7   To live the Christian life, a person will try to be patient and kind and forgiving.

8   To live the Christian life, a person will try to set bad things right.

9   To live the Christian life, a person will go on loving for ever—as God does.

10 To live the Christian life, a person will place their hope in God, trusting God's promises for the future.

11 To live the Christian life, a person will place their hope in a future with Jesus, and in doing the good things that will be worth something then.

12 To live the Christian life, a person needs to be ready at all times to explain why Jesus gives them hope even through the hard times.

13 The Christian life is based on three things: faith in God, hope for a future with God, and God's great love, to enjoy and to share.